Raised Bed Gardening

The complete beginners guide to build and grow your own vegetable garden. Make your backyard the starting point of your self-sufficiency path

CHAUNCEY CRUZ JR.

to Rosa and Mauro the Swimming Cap

© Copyright 2020 by *Chauncey Cruz jr*

All rights reserved.

This document is geared towards providing exact and reliable information with regards to the topic and issue covered. The publication is sold with the idea that the publisher is not required to render accounting, officially permitted, or otherwise, qualified services. If advice is necessary, legal or professional, a practiced individual in the profession should be ordered.

- From a Declaration of Principles which was accepted and approved equally by a Committee of the American Bar Association and a Committee of Publishers and Associations.

In no way is it legal to reproduce, duplicate, or transmit any part of this document in either electronic means or in printed format. Recording of this publication is strictly prohibited and any storage of this document is not allowed unless with written permission from the publisher. All rights reserved.

The information provided herein is stated to be truthful and consistent, in that any liability, in terms of inattention or otherwise, by any usage or abuse of any policies, processes, or directions contained within is the solitary and utter responsibility of the recipient reader. Under no circumstances will any legal responsibility or blame be held against the publisher for any reparation, damages, or monetary loss due to the information herein, either directly or indirectly.

Respective authors own all copyrights not held by the publisher.

The information herein is offered for informational purposes solely, and is universal as so. The presentation of the information is without contract or any type of guarantee assurance.

The trademarks that are used are without any consent, and the publication of the trademark is without permission or backing by the trademark owner. All trademarks and brands within this book are for clarifying purposes only and are the owned by the owners themselves, not affiliated with this document

Introduction	10
Enter: Raised Bed Gardening.	11
Chapter 1:	14
What is Raised Bed Gardening?	14
Where did it come from?	16
Let's do some Raised Bed Gardening	18
Chapter 2:	23
Why choose Raised Bed Gardening?	23
#1: RBG is ideal for beginners	24
#2: Better drainage	25
#3: You can plant earlier in the season	26
#4: Prevents long-term injury and pain	27
#5: Less weeding required	28
#6: Easier to maintain	29
#7: Add to aesthetic beauty of the garden	29
#8: Ideal for your old-age	30
#9: RBGs can be portable	31
#10: Safe from contaminated soil	32
#11: Maximize the available space	33

#12: Improve the soil underneath   34

Chapter 3: 36

How to build the raised bed 36

Points to consider before you begin   37

#1: Is it practical for you?   37

#2: What if you end up with Jack's Beanstalk?   38

#3: Are you willing to invest now and reap the rewards later?   39

#4: You might have to water it more frequently   40

#5: You will have to manage the spacing and layout   40

#6: Should you do it yourself or get external help?   41

Choosing the material for a raised bed   42

#1: Wood   43

#2: Bricks   45

#3: Stones, rocks, and flint   46

#4: Metal   47

#5: Natural materials   48

#6: Willow edging panels   49

#7: Recycled materials, or anything that you can find   51

The five basic tools   52

How high (or deep) should your raised bed be?   54

    Salad crops and herbs   56

    Herbaceous plants and vegetables   57

    Shrubs and fruit bushes   58

Finding a good location for your RBG   58

    The shade can be your friend   59

    The height changes where the sunlight falls   60

    Understanding the Sun's positions   61

    Thinking out of the box   62

    Some practical considerations   63

    Protection from wind is necessary   64

    Beware of the frost   66

6 easy steps for building a wooden raised bed   67

    #1: Find your spot and level out the ground   68

    #2: Mark the perimeter of the bed   68

    #3: Install the supporting stakes in the ground   69

    #4: Screw the wooden walls into place   70

    #5: Fill in some soil to form the base for your raised bed   70

    #6: Make up the top layer with quality topsoil and compost   71

8 easy steps to build a raised bed from bricks   72

#1: Find your spot and mark the perimeter	73
#2: Give it a concrete foundation	74
#3: Prepare the glue that will keep the bricks stuck together	75
#4: Let the bricks rise to the ground	75
#5: Let the bricks rise above the ground	76
#6: Make the top edge moisture-resistant and aesthetic	77
#7: Line the inside walls with a permeable membrane	77
#8: Fill it in with soil, topsoil, and compost	78

Chapter 4: How to plan your garden — 80

The types of soil that can go into your RBG	81
#1: Garden soil	81
#2: Potting mix	82
#3: Raised garden bed mix	82
#4: Topsoil	83
Soil pH and nutrients	84
Acidic of alkaline?	84
What are the essential nutrients?	85
Compost and peat moss – essential partners for your soil	86
What is compost?	87
What is peat moss?	88

Which one should you use?	89
When should I add the compost every year?	91
From seed to seedling and plant	92
Harden your seeds with indoor sowing	93
Skip the indoor step and sow them directly	95
Grooming the seedlings	96

Chapter 5: Factors that determine what and how you plant 97

Season	98
Preference for sunlight and water	99
Location	99
Companion Vegetables	100

Chapter 6: the 5 Best vegetables to grow 103

#1: Tomatoes	104
#2: Cucumbers	105
#3: Garlic	106
#4: Leaf lettuce	107
#5: Summer squash	108

Chapter 7: the 6 best herbs to grow 110

#1: Basil	110
#2: Greek oregano	111

#3: Rosemary 112

#4: Thyme 113

#5: Mint 114

#6: Parsley 115

Chapter 8: Importance of post-harvest care — **116**

#1: Finish your harvest 117

#2: Remove the summer and diseased plants, and weeds 117

#3: Replenish your soil's nutrients 118

#4: Cover the surface 119

#5: Give the perennials their due 119

#6: Your garden tools need your attention 119

#7: Prepare for next year 120

Chapter 9: Protecting the plants from pests — **121**

#1: Gather a team of beneficial insects to help you out! 122

#2: Choose pest-resistant varieties 123

#3: Install physical barriers 123

#4: Intercropping will confuse the pests 124

#5: Focus on the health of your plants 125

Chapter 10: 5 Common mistakes and how to avoid them 127

#1: Your raised beds are too wide	128
#2: You didn't plan the irrigation well	128
#3: The material of your RBG is unsafe	129
#4: The soil lacks nutrients	130
#5: RBGs are placed too close to each other	131
Conclusion	**133**
References	**134**

Introduction

Gardening is a practice that takes a lot of patience, care, and hard work, but is so rewarding and fulfilling that anyone who starts out instantly falls in love with it. There is something magical about watching a small seed that you planted and took care of blossom and grow into a big plant bearing all kinds of fruits and vegetables. It brings us closest to nature and life itself, because it is nature allowing us to participate in its work, giving us the opportunity to bring life out of mere potential.

In recent years, people have become increasingly passionate with the idea of 'growing your own vegetables', a feat that our centuries old ancestors found standard practice. With all the pesticides and chemicals that go into producing vegetables on commercial farms, and the number of times these vegetables change hands before getting to us, we are bound to worry about the state of the produce, and our own health.

What makes the idea of becoming self-sufficient even more attractive is the development of techniques that make the process a whole lot easier. Previously, if you wanted to raise vegetables in your own garden, you would have had to worry about having an adequate layer of good quality soil so that the roots can go deep and provide a good foundation for the plant. You would have had to worry about the soil getting compacted beneath your feet as you move around the garden watering the plants. There was a lot to worry about which made the process all the more exhausting.

Enter: *Raised Bed Gardening.*

Raised Bed Gardening, or RBG for short, is a technique in which plants are grown in small and elevated containers that are walled on all sides. This allows you to pack in a tall column of good quality soil for each plant, allowing the roots to grow deep and strong. Among other things, this technique has the potential to solve your back pain problems.

However, RBG is not something that you can just start out with on a whim. It requires you to first properly understand the principles of gardening and growing vegetables in raised beds, it requires you to know what to grow and what not to grow, and most importantly, it requires you to know how to build a proper raised bed.

People tend to avoid the pain of sitting down, learning, and planning before actually starting out with RBG. This leads to massive disappointments because they are able to reap none of its benefits and find it to be quite difficult.

That is why I have written this book. In the chapters that follow, I have compiled and distilled in an easy-to-follow manner all the information that you will ever need to develop a good understanding of Raised Bed Gardening, and go on to successfully harvest fresh and healthy vegetables using this technique.

I have covered topics ranging from the different types of beds and the various methods to build raised beds all the way to the vegetables that you can grow and the pitfalls that you should avoid. You do not need to think of this as a thick and complicated book that will take you ages to read from cover to cover. The book is structured in a reader-friendly way, and you can use the table of contents to jump to any section of the book which you find is more important to you at the moment.

In the end, I congratulate you on taking the first step towards a self-sufficient and healthy future, and wish you the best of luck in your journey as you grow the best vegetables in your own garden. I hope you enjoy going through this book as much as I enjoyed writing it for you!

Chapter 1:
What is Raised Bed Gardening?

Raised Bed Gardening (RBG) is a type of gardening technique that involves growing plants in an elevated enclosure of soil which is quite often enriched with compost and manure.

The enclosure or containment unit is generally three to four feet in width and can have a height ranging from 6 inches (slightly above the ground) to waist-level, depending on the type of plant that you intend to grow. The unit is filled with soil which lays on top of the actual garden bed and holds the roots of the plants. The edges of the 'bed' can be made of any non-toxic material – wood, concrete, marble, stones, bricks, and even sturdy plastic – anything that you can easily lay your hands on and fix in place [1].

The beds can be of various shapes; you could have square, rectangular, hexagonal, and even round-edged beds in which you grow your plants. Recently, a number of companies and gardening enthusiasts have started selling 'kits' for RBG: ready-to-install structures that take less than an hour to properly fix in your garden, saving you all the hassle of finding the materials to make the edges. These kits can also include specially prepared organic soil which you can pour directly inside the bed. This soil is not as heavy as standard topsoil and its suitable texture allows the plants to blossom freely and fully.

RBGs are generally placed along walkways and paths in order to make it easier to tend to the plants and water them. You can grow a wide range of fruits and vegetables in them including tomatoes, lettuce, garlic chives, pansies, peppers, and many varieties of herbs!

Where did it come from?

It is always quite intriguing to trace the origin and development of a concept. The concept of having a 'raised platform' on which to grow plants existed as far back as the medieval times, when gardeners built the edges of their growing soil using wattle fences.

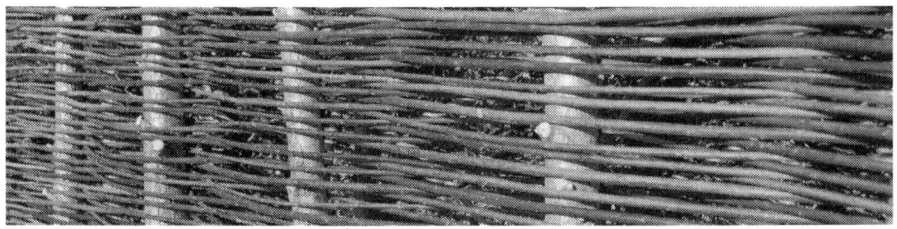

Even in the 18th century it was common to see the gardeners of Paris packing their plots up with the manure lying around from all the horses (which were the main way of transportation back then) that dominated the streets [2]. There was so much compost at hand that the beds could reach up to as much as two meters in height!

The concept gained the most momentum in the 1970s, when farmers started digging up paths between rounded 'mounds' of soil on which they would grow plants. The idea was that by not walking on these mounds (and using the paths instead), the soil would remain soft and not become compacted, thus allowing for better absorption of water and nutrients. The only time you would have to step on top of them would be during the cultivation, weeding, and harvesting season of the crops.

However, this technique failed whenever it rained heavily, because the excess soil from the mound would get washed over into the paths, leveling to the ground and frustrating the purpose of the mound. The same would happen during the cultivation period, i.e. the ground would go back to normal and you would have to dig up the mounds again before the next crops were planted.

This is when the concept of having a strong, 'walled' enclosure crept into the mainstream. By surrounding the mounds with a sturdy structure, you compromised on the area available for planting, but ultimately benefited from the stability of the mound, even in times of heavy rain.

This innovation got adapted into various forms because it was an ideal way to grow plants in a garden where you have limited space and not a very good layer of soil. Over time, this practice became known as Raised Bed Gardening, and here we are, taking it forward.

Let's do some Raised Bed Gardening

Now that you have a basic overview of what RBG is and understand how it was developed, it is time to take a deep dive into each of the steps leading up to a full-fledged raised bed garden which will supply you with fresh vegetables and fruits!

To help you with the exploration, I've provided a brief outline of the subsequent chapters below. If you're someone who wants to follow the steps from the first right down to the last one, the list will prime you for all the knowledge that you will be taking in, giving you a solid framework to build upon. If you are simply someone looking for guidance regarding a specific step (e.g. about harvesting and post-harvest care), the list will point you in the right direction.

Chapter 2: Why RBG?

If you are still on the fence about whether you should try RBG out or stick with traditional gardening, this chapter will quell all of your fears by giving you twelve advantages of choosing raised bed gardening.

Chapter 3: How to build a raised bed

This is one of the most important chapters in this book. It contains information about the types of raised beds, the materials that can be used, the tools you will need, and a step by step breakdown of how you can build your own raised bed.

Chapter 4: Planning the garden

This chapter will teach you: the various types of soil that a plant can grow in and which type is ideal for RBG; how to select the peat moss, compost, fertilizers, and how to go about the seeding.

Chapter 5: How to choose what to plant

As the title already explains, this chapter will describe the factors you need to consider when deciding what to plant. You will also find neatly tabulated information about companion vegetable groups.

Chapter 6: The vegetables

This chapter contains a list of 5 easy-to-grow vegetables with their characteristics and growing techniques.

Chapter 7: Growing herbs

A list of 6 herbs, their characteristics, and growing techniques.

Chapter 8: Harvest and post-harvest care

Harvesting will get you the fruit of your labor, but post-harvest care will make sure that you do not end up ruining your raised bed garden, making it incapable of use. This chapter will give you the 7 things you need to do to get better produce year after year.

Chapter 9: Protecting the plants from pest

Pests can quickly lay waste to months of hard work and effort. This chapter will equip you with the knowledge to help you protect your plants from pests.

Chapter 10: Common mistakes and how to avoid them

Finally, a compilation of all the common pitfalls that people have fallen into while trying out RBG, so that you can learn from their mistakes and reap the benefits!

Let's begin!

Chapter 2:
Why choose Raised Bed Gardening?

It may be the case that this is the first time you are hearing about RBG, or maybe you already know quite a lot of people who have adopted it as their primary method and you want to know what the hype is all about. This chapter will help you clear your mind and ultimately decide whether you want to go down this road or not, by giving you twelve solid advantages of RBG. Without further ado, let's jump right in:

#1: RBG is ideal for beginners

If you are someone who is only just starting out with gardening, trying out RBG will greatly ease the learning process for you. Compared to traditional gardening, RBG takes away a lot of the difficulties and simplifies the entire process, increasing the chances that your efforts will result in a tall and healthy plant.

The process will be as simple as building a raised bed, filling in the right soil, sowing the seeds, making sure the plant is watered frequently, weeding it when necessary, and there you have it: your seed will grow into a healthy fruit - and vegetable - bearing plant. This will save you from all the confusing and never-ending cycles of tilling, weeding, and fertilizing that are a part and parcel of traditional gardening [3].

#2: Better drainage

The height of the raised bed is a factor that plays very nicely to our advantage. With the soil resting at a height above the ground and not getting compacted by people walking on top of it, water is easily able to seep through the pores in the soil and reach the roots.

This is particularly beneficial in places that experience great amounts of flooding because the raised beds will allow much better drainage of the flood water, while at the same time giving your plants some breathing room above the level of the water because of the height. In some areas, this may be the only technique that would allow a full year's cultivation and harvest.

#3: You can plant earlier in the season

Following on from the previous advantage, having better drainage characteristics means that during spring your raised bed will be able to drain away the water and become warm much faster than the soil on the ground. This means that you can plant your seeds much earlier than you would if you were planting it in the ground.

Moreover, because the soil is able to regulate temperatures more effectively, there is a higher chance that most of your plants will survive extreme winter conditions and come out of it alive and ready to thrive. Note that the quality and state of the soil plays an important role in enabling this, because you can only expect these results if the soil is untilled and enriched with compost [4].

#4: Prevents long-term injury and pain

If you have spent a lot of time doing traditional gardening, you must know the debilitating back and knee pain that comes as a result of spending long periods of time bending down while tilling and weeding the soil. Unless anything is done about this pain, the constant stress on your back and joints can cause potential long-term injuries, making it difficult for you to maintain a proper posture once you start getting old.

Having a bed raised to waist-level can solve this problem for good, because with RBG you no longer need to bend down and arch your back in order to weed and take care of the soil. This is a lot safer for the long-term, especially for youngsters who are considering a life in gardening. Implementing RBG from the beginning can make sure they end their lives with a healthy back and functioning knee.

#5: Less weeding required

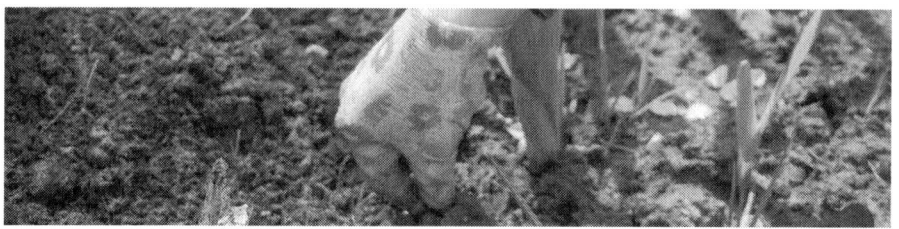

Weeding is one of the most important and time-taking processes when it comes to gardening. The very act of tilling allows small weed seeds to get trapped inside the soil, eventually growing up to cause a lot of problems if not dealt with.

With RBG, there is no need to till the soil and so there is a much smaller chance of weeds growing out of nowhere. Even if they do during the winter, you can cover them up with an opaque covering that blocks sunlight, causing them to die away.

You can then rake them out before you are planting your seeds in spring.

#6: Easier to maintain

Do you know that moment when you step out to maintain your garden, only to feel overwhelmed by the limitless planting area in front of you?

RBGs fix this problem because they divide the garden up into small, discrete chunks which you can tackle one at a time. This seems a lot easier to do psychologically because you can focus on one specific bed at a time and complete it, getting a sense of accomplishing something, before moving on to the next. Before you know it, you have completed all the RBGs and your entire garden area is up-to-date.

#7: Add to aesthetic beauty of the garden

Your raised bed garden does not have to look like someone forcefully inserted an old wooden carton into the ground and filled it up with soil. There is so much you can do to make your raised bed visually appealing and attractive.

You can go creative by varying the height of the beds, arranging them into some architectural form that looks beautiful and yet does not hamper the safe and sound growth of your plants. You can take a paint brush and color the edges in whatever pattern you want to.

#8: Ideal for your old-age

This advantage follows from the fact we discussed earlier about raised bed gardening being safe for your long-term health and mobility. When people get old, it becomes a lot more difficult for them to bend down to perform physically intensive activities. This is one of the reasons that people stop gardening as they get older – their backs and knees no longer allow them to.

If you invest in RBG from the start, you can make sure to be gardening and growing delicious fruits and vegetables well into your old age when other people of your age are giving it up. You can also think of this as a good way of getting your old parents or grandparents to develop a good hobby that keeps them close to nature and healthy all the time.

#9: RBGs can be portable

Let's say that you are living in a rented house and really want to have a garden where you can grow your own vegetables. It would be quite difficult for you to have a standard garden because the decision ultimately lies with your landlord. They may not like all the messy soil, dirt, broken leaves, and worms crawling about their property because of your passion for gardening.

This is where a raised bed garden can save your day. All you have to do is get a sturdy and securely enclosed raised bed and cover its insides with cardboard to prevent the soil from getting out. Pour in the soil and invite your landlord for a demonstration. You will definitely be able to convince them that if they were to ask you to clear out the property the very next day, you'd simply carry the RBG straight out of the house without leaving any trace of it.

This is a greatly useful advantage for people who are living in urban settings and may not necessarily have a garden on which to make a raised bed. They can simply get a closed RBG that is covered from below and place it on an empty piece of concrete, moving it to some other location whenever needed. You cannot move an entire garden, but you can surely transport an RBG.

#10: Safe from contaminated soil

The last thing you would want is for you or your family to ingest toxic heavy metals from supposedly 'fresh', 'healthy', and 'homegrown' vegetables. However, if you are an urban gardener, you may be at risk of heavy metals contaminating the soil on which you grow your plants. This could be because of materials like lead seeping into your soil from the nearest road, an ever present feature of urban cities.

It can get quite difficult to make sure you are safe from contamination: you will have to position your garden away from the roads, research about past uses of your land to make sure nothing toxic touched the soil on which you're planting, and plant thick hedges to prevent the contaminants from getting to your vegetable plants.

Raised bed gardens can make this situation a whole lot easier. All you will have to do is fill in your raised beds with new soil that you know is free of all contaminants. Since it will never come into contact with the soil underneath, you will not have to worry even the tiniest bit about contaminants making their way through the vegetables into the mouths of your family members. A simple solution that makes all the hard effort unnecessary.

#11: Maximize the available space

It should not come as a surprise that RBG allows you to achieve greater yield per square feet as compared to traditional on-ground gardening. To put it simply, two gardens of the same size but one with a raised bed and one in-ground will produce different amounts of vegetables for you. The raised bed will deliver more.

The reason behind this can be a bit difficult to intuit. After all, both are using the same area, no? The key lies in the depth of soil available for raised bed gardens. The layer of soil on the ground does not go deep and so roots have to spread out a lot more, covering a larger area to get the nutrients that are needed. On the other hand, the roots of plants in raised beds are kept inside soil that runs deep, allowing the roots to reach further down in order to grow and absorb nutrients. As a result, you can place the plants much closer together in raised beds as compared to in-ground beds without sacrificing the health of the plants. Talk about getting more bang for your buck!

#12: Improve the soil underneath

In places where the soil is unsuitable for growing any kind of plant, or if you have a patio garden and therefore no soil at all, making a raised bed garden can do wonders for you, and your soil. The RBG will improve the quality of the soil in your garden and help you cultivate plants which are not remotely suitable for it, such as alpines and lime-intolerant plants.

This brings us to the end of this exhaustive list of benefits! I hope you enjoyed going through each of them, and felt your desire to get started with your own raised bed reinforced. Now, to get you started and guide you on the crucial steps of building a raised bed garden, the next chapter will take a deep dive into the ins and outs of constructing a raised bed garden. Let's get started!

Chapter 3:
How to build the raised bed

This chapter is one of the most important chapters in this entire book because there are so many combinations that you can go for when building a raised bed, and so many materials to choose among. What you choose will ultimately determine whether you will be able to pull RBG off successfully, or not.

Therefore, we will be going over some important considerations, the tools and materials needed, the design, the size, location, alternatives, and practical instructions – in short, everything related to building a raised bed compiled into one chapter. If you are already experienced and just looking for ideas, you do not need to read everything cover to cover since it will be sufficient for you to navigate to your desired section and read through it. Let's begin.

Points to consider before you begin

Just like everything else, RBG is not something that invites you to simply pick up all the tools and materials and get started. Even before you go buy the materials, you have to consider a few aspects that can affect your experience of raised bed gardening.

#1: Is it practical for you?

One of the benefits of raised bed gardening is that you don't have to strain your back, trying to bend over to reach the soil and plants. However, this can be a double edged sword. With a raised bed, you will not have to bend over, but if you plan to use a watering can, you will have to lift it to a greater height. This can strain the back and your shoulders if you are not careful. If you feel that this will be a difficulty for you, consider installing a hose with a spray nozzle at the end – that will solve all of your problems.

Moreover, instead of hauling compost and other materials in wheelbarrows (as you would if your garden was on the ground), load the mixtures into lighter containers such as buckets whenever you have to reload the soil in your raised bed gardens.

#2: What if you end up with Jack's Beanstalk?

Raised bed gardens allow plants and vegetables to grow at a height so that it is much easier for you to harvest them since these will be anywhere between waist-level or even up to your face.

But what if you are planning to plant French and runner beans, or hops? These plants grow to a great height and might actually grow so tall that you would have to stand on a stool or ladder in order to harvest them. Do not worry if you really do want to plant these crops – certain dwarf versions of these plants are available which you can grow, maintain, and harvest quite easily!

#3: Are you willing to invest now and reap the rewards later?

Undertaking raised bed gardening is not the cheapest method in the world, especially compared to gardening in the ground-soil. The very first expenditure that you will have to face is that of the materials and tools that you will need to construct your raised bed. The actual cost will vary based on whether you make a lumbar, brick-walled, or masonry-based raised bed.

Moreover, some people might have some high quality compost lying around, but that is not the case with everyone. Most people, when starting out with RBG, will need to spend on some high quality soil and compost mixture to use, which can be bought in excess and stored for later replenishing. However, you should not be dissuaded because of these expenses. This initial 'investment' will be offset through longer years, a longer harvesting season, and freedom from slug and insect protection.

Overall, the efficiency of RBG will make you forget all the money that you put into it.

#4: You might have to water it more frequently

The 'raised' nature of the beds means that the water that you pour from the top will drain through quite efficiently because of the excellent drainage characteristics. This means that you will have to water RBGs a lot more frequently than you would water a normal garden with soil on the ground. However, there are certain configurations and techniques that allow the soil to retain moisture rather than losing it. We will be looking at those in the upcoming sections.

#5: You will have to manage the spacing and layout

You cannot cover your entire land area with raised bed gardens because you cannot walk on top of a RBG. Therefore, you will ultimately have less space than traditional gardens to use for the plantation, keeping the remaining space aside for the paths and walkways.

As a general guideline, you should leave enough space between RBGs to allow for a wheelbarrow to be moved around, carrying compost which will be poured inside the beds. This reduced space should not be a matter of worry for you, however, because you can make up for it by planting your vegetables a lot closer together in the beds owing to the increased soil depth and drainage. In fact, this could be an advantage for you if you are someone who likes to keep things structured.

#6: Should you do it yourself or get external help?

If the ordeal seems a bit too complicated for you, you could always go ahead and hire a landscape gardener to build your raised beds for you and get you started with the planting. You could even buy commercially available DIY Raised Bed kits that are easy to assemble and install, but which come with additional costs. Ultimately, I would advise you to take the courageous step forward and build your raised bed yourself using our guide. Not just will it save you a lot of money, you will become experienced enough to do it again, whenever needed.

Those were the six points that you need to keep in mind before you get started out. Once you have that sorted out and are looking to build your own raised bed, the very next thing to do would be to decide on the material you will use to make your bed. Let's now look at all the materials that you can use, along with some precautions.

Choosing the material for a raised bed

There is a wide range of materials that you can use to construct your raised bed, with the condition being that it is strong enough to hold its position against a bed of soil for years on end.

Another important factor that you should take care of nowadays is that the material does not contaminate the soil. Old railroad ties are known to release accumulated tar into the soil, damaging it significantly. Some treated kinds of wood leach arsenic and other toxic chemicals into the soil, and these toxins can potentially end up inside your own body through the plants that you will grow in that soil.

Therefore, once you've made sure of the above, you need only consider the cost, availability, and longevity of the materials (along with your own aesthetic sense!) when deciding the materials to use. Let's now look at the list of materials that you can choose from.

#1: Wood

Wood is the cheapest and also the most easily available material that you can use for building your raised beds. On top of that, you only need to have basic DIY skills along with a drill, hammer, and some screws in order to put together your raised bed. There are several varieties of wood that you can use:

- Hardwood

- Softwood: less durable than hardwood unless pressure treated

- Gravel boards: light and strong, and can be stacked up if you want to raise the height later on

- Railroad ties: you can get these from lumbar merchants and they will turn out to be sturdy and attractive-looking for your raised bed

- Logs: tree surgeons and garden companies often have excess logs with them, so you can approach them if you want to go ahead with these

As you can see, wood offers a variety of choices, with each giving a different visual appeal to your raised beds. However, there is one drawback to using wood: any bed made out of wood will eventually rot away after a few years and will need to be replaced, so you will have to spend money on making a new wooden bed after some time. Therefore, if you are going with wood, go for a cheap bed that will last you the longest, so that you don't feel too heavy spending again after some years.

#2: Bricks

Although you will need some bricklaying skills and will have to take care of a couple of other features, you will solve most of your problems if you decide to go ahead with using bricks for your raised bed. Bricks are tough and durable, and if houses are any measure to go by, a raised bed made out of bricks will last for years on end.

The two things you have to be careful about include providing a solid footing to the brick-walls in order to stop them from sinking and coming apart, and installing a capping layer at the top in order to prevent the water from leaking out. If you take care of this, a raised bed made out of bricks will serve you well for many years.

In order to make it blend into the general outlook of your house, you can find bricks that have a similar color to the exterior of your house. However, there is one caveat to using bricks – unless you already have some lying around, you will have to go buy them, and bricks turn out to be expensive. Even though the initial investment will pay off in the form of a long service duration, you can search recycling stores and construction sites for excess or available bricks that you can use for your bed.

#3: Stones, rocks, and flint

This is one of the most convenient and cheapest alternatives if you have some adequately sized stones and rocks lying around in your garden. You can utilize these to form the walls of your raised beds, but you will have to work out a solution for the spaces and crevices that are left between these rocks and stones.

A possible solution for this would be to utilize cement, or a lime-based mortar to fill in the spaces and create a solid, impenetrable wall. Not only will this cost you much less than bricks, this will last a lot longer than if your bed was made of wood.

#4: Metal

Yes, metal has made its way to this list as well. Given its versatility, metal can be a stylish and pleasing material to use for making the walls of your raised bed. A big advantage is its availability – you can find a lot of metal lying around in scrapyards or retrieve it from appliances or objects that you are not using anymore. You can even have a metal worker or engineering company give you custom-sized sheets or plates for you to use.

The only thing that you will have to take care of is the temperature – the metal bed will get quite hot in the summer and so you will have to water your bed a lot more than normal, and there is a similar situation for winter: the metal bed could get quite cold, hampering the effectiveness of the soil, ultimately reducing the quality of your plants. As long as you can take care of these issues (or live in a moderate climate without significant temperature variation), you are good to go!

#5: Natural materials

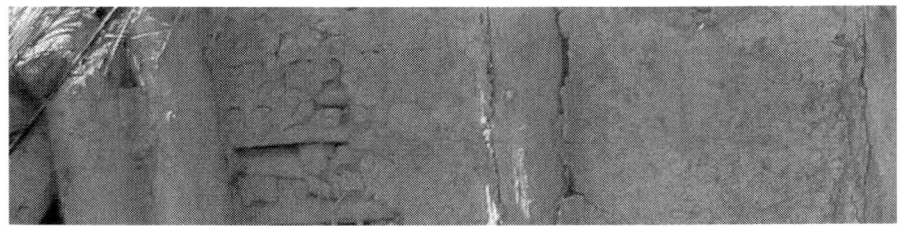

Materials such as wattle and daub are used to make walls for houses, and so using it to make your raised bed is an idea you can explore if you can easily get your hands on it. More of such natural materials include sod, and soil that is packed into a retaining wall – all of these combinations can work well if you want to avoid using the more costly materials like metal and bricks.

The only thing to keep in mind with these materials is that although they may look pleasing to the eye, they have a short life and you will have to replace them almost every couple of years.

#6: Willow edging panels

Willow edging panels are not only conveniently available online (because they are used in kitchen gardens for their aesthetic value), they can also be an easy option if you do not plan on having very high raised beds. These panels have to be installed on wooden stakes inserted into the ground at appropriate places to bring structural integrity to the entire bed, but do not make the mistake of relying too much on them: if you go above 10 inches in height, there is a real chance that your raised bed will tumble to the ground because of the weight of the soil inside.

These panels are made from natural material which is not treated, and so you can expect beds made out of these to last you a few years, but you can increase the lifespan if you are only interested in annual harvesting: put them inside during the winter and install them back again at the end of winter. In the end, if you do not want to rely on them to bring strength to your raised bed, you can use them to improve the visual appeal of your raised bed by lining these panels on the outside of the walls of your raised bed.

#7: Recycled materials, or anything that you can find

Human creativity knows no bounds, and if you find yourself hesitating at the effort involved in using any of the above materials, you can turn to your own creativity for help. Search your house and shed for anything sturdy that can be pushed into the ground, or something that has natural borders and can contain soil inside. Some possibilities include: a rubber tire, roof tiles, and even the abandoned chassis of a car.

It must have gotten clear to you by now that you have a lot of options to choose from, and you don't necessarily have to splurge a lot of cash in order to have a nice and effective raised bed for your garden. All you need is some scavenging skills and a good helping of creativity!

Now that you have an idea of the material that you should be choosing for your RBG, let's now take a quick look at some of the tools that you will need to build your raised bed.

The five basic tools

The most common material that people tend to use to make their raised bed is wood, particularly because it is the cheapest option available and the process of building a raised bed with it is quite convenient. Therefore, in this book, we will explore building two kinds of raised beds: a lumber raised bed, and one made with bricks.

Here are the five tools that you should have on hand (or rent, if possible) when you start building your bed:

1. Hand saw:

You might not necessarily get custom-sized logs or wood planks from the merchant, or you might have some lying around in your house which you are thinking of utilizing for the bed. The hand saw will help you cut them to the appropriate size and length, helping you clear out the unevenness and make sure all the pieces fit snugly together.

2. Carpenter's Square:

You do not want your bed to look like an injured rectangle, instead of a crisp one with accurate ninety degree angles. The carpenter's square will help you make sure of this.

3. Level gauge:

It is important that the soil you fill inside your bed is level on the top, in order to prevent the water from flowing in one direction and starving a section of the soil from it. The same is true for the panels that will form the structure for the bed. The level gauge will show you the deviations (if there are) and help you fix them.

4. Drill:

You cannot join the lumbar panels of your bed using some kind of wood glue – it could leak into the soil, affecting the quality and health of your plants. A better way to join the corners would be to use screws, and the drill will help you make the holes for those to be inserted.

5. Screw driver

As mentioned above, it is best to use screws to join the wooden panels from the corners, because this will keep your frame sturdy and solid, preventing it from unnecessary wobbling and sinking.

Those were the five most important tools you will need when starting out with building your own wooden raised bed. Let's now head over to the next section and figure out what factors you need to consider when deciding on the depth of your bed.

How high (or deep) should your raised bed be?

The answer to this question depends on a number of factors:

- Type of plant you want to grow
- The base of your raised bed

We will discuss how the type of plant affects the recommended depth in the following paragraphs, however it is a good opportunity to discuss how the base of the bed factors in.

If you are growing your bed on a patio, there will not be any soil below the base of your bed, and so this means that you will have to keep a high bed to provide your plants enough depth to spread and grow their roots. The same applies if you are keeping your bed in a garden but giving it a solid base – your bed will have to be generally higher.

For the former situation, there really isn't anything that you can do. But if you are making your raised bed in a garden and you want to give it a base, consider laying a chicken net instead of a solid foundation, or having no base altogether. This will effectively increase the amount of soil that your plants have, particularly in the case of having no base at all – this will allow you to build a bed with a smaller height than normal because the soil in the garden (beneath the bed's base) will be available for your plants to reach down into. In this case, it doesn't really matter what height you choose for your bed.

Let's now take a look at the different kinds of plants you can grow and the recommended depth for each:

Salad crops and herbs

Salad crops are not quite ambitious, which means that it is sufficient to have even a 4 inch high raised bed if you want to grow them. Because of their shallow rooting, you can keep your raised bed low and still get moderately-sized and high-quality leaves. This is not a strict rule, however, because you may have a completely different reason for having a high raised bed: maybe you want to bend over less and protect your back, maybe you want it to match the height of other raised beds.

Moreover, the same applies to a number of round-the-year herbs such as thyme, rosemary, and mint, which originate from the Mediterranean region and can grow in arid climates and poor conditions. The choice is ultimately yours, but remember that you can keep it low if these are the only crops you want to grow.

Herbaceous plants and vegetables

Certain herbaceous perennials that grow in a cycle every year have deeper and denser roots, and so will require you to build a deeper bed than if you were planting salad crops.

The same goes for vegetables like carrots, potatoes, cabbages, peas, beans, and so on. These will also produce deep roots and the recommended raised bed height if you want to grow these is at least 12 inches. This will make sure that these grow to their full potential.

If you cannot accommodate 12 inches, you can still plant them in lower beds but you will have to take extra care of them, watering and feeding them a lot more frequently than you would otherwise, in order to compensate for the limited growing space.

Shrubs and fruit bushes

The recommended raised bed depth to allow shrubs and fruit bushes to fully develop and grow is at least 20 inches. Again, as was the case with vegetables, you can attempt to grow shrubs and fruit bushes in a smaller bed but it will need extra care, may end up stunted, and will most likely wither away earlier than if there was a bit more depth of soil available.

Now that you have understood how you can go about deciding on the height of the raised beds, let's now turn to the next question: where should you locate your raised bed?

Finding a good location for your RBG

Plants are living beings, just like us humans, and so the weather and conditions they are kept in affect their development and quality. Just like we need food to fuel our bodies and continue to function normally, plants need sunlight to carry out their basic processes and survive and grow. Of course, the amount of sunlight needed varies from type to type, and so the key in getting the right location for your raised bed garden is to pair the right kind of plant with the right location. Of course, it may be that your choices are limited, but there are some guidelines that you should follow nonetheless. Let's take a look at these.

The shade can be your friend

It is true that plants generally enjoy being in a lot of sunlight, and so it is best if you can find an open and sunny site in which to locate your RBGs. This allows the plants to carry out a lot more photosynthesis, making glucose, which adds to the sweet flavor of fruits.

However, if your hands are tied and you find yourself forced to place some RBGs in shady corners, you do not need to worry. There are actually some plant varieties that can thrive well even without too much direct sunlight. For example, leafy plants such as cabbages, spinach, lettuce, and other summer salads do just fine in shady areas as well. In fact, the absence of direct sunlight will prevent the soil from drying out very quickly, making the roots cooler and the vegetables less likely to burn out because of lack of moisture.

Finally, if you are good with planting some ornamental crops, you can find certain varieties such as ferns, hostas, epimediums, and hellebores which can grow well in shady areas.

The height changes where the sunlight falls

Of course, the first thing you would do (if you weren't going to already) is to scan your garden properly and identify the right places which receive the most amount of sunlight – that is where you would locate your RBGs, right?

Turns out, there is a slight catch. This strategy would have worked out perfectly if you were planting on the ground, but that is the key difference, your plants are going to be elevated. Once you raise the height of a bed and plant, it might be possible that even though the ground at that location receives a lot of sunlight, the plant (which is higher up) does not. This can wreck the development of your garden if you are not careful about it.

Moreover, you also need to be wary of tree canopies, walls, and roofs, because these might end up blocking sunlight for your RBG plants.

Understanding the Sun's positions

The Sun is not a globe of light that just hangs in the sky, fixed in the same position before switching off when the night rolls around. In fact, it rises from the East and sets in the West, staying in the South direction for the major part of its trip.

Therefore, you should spend some time considering the position of your garden – ideally, you want your plants to be facing South so that they can receive the maximum possible amount of sunlight every day. This might not be possible for you, but figure out the window in your garden during which your plants will be able to receive the maximum sunlight, and place them accordingly. If your backyard faces the North but you have a front-yard as well, consider placing your RBGs in the front yard to benefit from the sunlight available there.

Thinking out of the box

If you feel that your garden is starved of sunlight, then instead of trying to make the best of what is available, you can try to increase the amount of sunlight that you are getting. You can do this by cutting down the height of the boundary fences around your house, which will allow more sunlight to fall on your garden, but this might come at the expense of your privacy, so it is up to you to assess the feasibility.

Another way to get more light is to clear out any overhanging and overgrown vegetation that is blocking the sunlight from reaching your garden. Moreover, you can even ask your neighbors if it is possible for them to reduce the height of their boundary or cut down their trees a little so that some sunlight can reach your garden. You may offer some of the future products of your garden in exchange for their kindness. Remember, there is no guarantee that any of these ideas will work out, but if they do, you will definitely see a difference in the amount of sunlight that your garden is getting!

Some practical considerations

There are some practical reasons other than sunlight which will help you in deciding where and how to site your RBGs. Let's take a look at some examples:

- If you are growing vegetables or herbs, it makes sense to have your plants growing close to the kitchen or in the back yard so that they are easily accessible and you can just go and pluck out some fresh veggies when you need some.

- If you want to increase the level of privacy in your house (or your garden), you can place raised beds near the outside edges of your garden so that the plants will act as walls, letting you do whatever you want to do in your home without your neighbors poking their noses into your matters.

- Planting some raised beds around a patio or seating area can be a good idea if you want to raise the level of privacy, making the people sitting there feel a lot more secure.

- Finally, it would be a bad idea to plant your raised beds too close to your house because you do not want the plants blocking the outside view from your windows, stopping you from having tabs on what is going on outside.

So as you can see, there are reasons that play a role in helping you decide where to locate your raised beds, such as the ones presented above. This is not an exhaustive list and depending on how your house and garden are set up, there can be other reasons for you to consider. The key is to integrate these raised beds with another useful function or convenience, instead of letting them sit haphazardly in your garden.

Protection from wind is necessary

Plants are delicate beings, and as such, require protection from the strong forces of nature, especially wind. Not only can a strong gust of wind break the plant and ruin its leaves, it can also take away the moisture from the soil, reducing your yield and quality during the peak growth seasons. There are several ways you can prevent this from happening.

One obvious solution if you live in a windy place is to select plant varieties that can survive these strong winds – you can look towards those that grow well in coastal climates for this. However, if you are specific about what you want to grow (and are planting tender vegetable and fruit plants), you need to work out a way to break the force of the wind.

If your garden is already surrounded by walls, fences, and hedges, you need not worry too much because these structures will be able to act as windbreakers and will protect your plants from getting damaged. Moreover, if your garden is on an elevated piece of land already, it would be best to reconsider the idea of having raised beds – the winds will not take mercy on your plants at all.

That said, if you need to install a windbreaker, you should go with hedges. Hedges are quite effective since they break the flow of the wind but do not obstruct it completely, allowing enough air circulation to keep your plants safe from pests and insects. Walls and fences, on the other hand, can become counter-productive, blocking the wind but creating accumulation near the top edges that can descend on your raised beds with vengeful force.

Beware of the frost

Just like the wind, frost and cold pockets can severely damage your plants. For stems only just sprouting out of the seeds, it will spell instant death, whereas it will gradually cripple your larger plants that have managed to develop out of the soil.

'Frost pockets' generally form in the lowest area of your garden, because the warm air gets displaced by the cold winds which ends up making the pockets its home. Therefore, you need to be wary of any such threat and make sure that your plants are kept safe from the cold.

The downside of this is that frost will greatly shorten your season, i.e. you will not be able to plant early and your plants will end up withering away sooner than you would like. If there is no way that you can deal with a certain frost pocket, you should then adapt to it and plant late in the season in order to prevent your plant from dying away.

By now, you must be thinking: will we ever get to the actual building of a raised bed part, or are we going to spend the rest of the book talking about other important things? Here is the good news: we are finally there!

Of course, it was incredibly important that you understand all that I've just talked about before you start building your bed, which is why all of that material was kept before the actual instructions. However, now that you are ready and prepared, let's get down to business.

6 easy steps for building a wooden raised bed

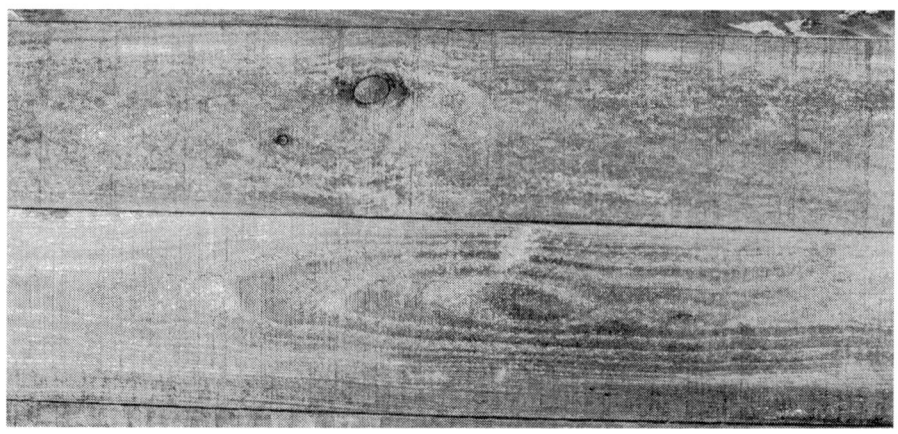

As mentioned earlier, we will be looking at the two most common types of raised beds: wooden, and brick-based. In this section, I have broken the process of making a wooden raised bed down into 6 simple steps that you need to follow. Let's dive right in!

#1: Find your spot and level out the ground

Needless to say, the first thing that you will have to do is to decide where you want to make your raised bed. This could be on a patio, but for most cases, it will be in your garden (recall the benefits of having a good quality soil foundation). Mark out the area and dig the excess soil from the top, especially if there is grass growing on it. Remember, if the soil is of a good quality, you can save it for later use, so do not dispose of it immediately.

#2: Mark the perimeter of the bed

Once you know where you want to make your RBG, the next thing you have to do is take a string or a rope, anything that you can mark out the perimeter of your raised bed with. Remember that you will have to decide on the actual width and length of your bed, based on your own convenience and based on the layout of your garden. Try not to make your raised bed too wide, because that will make it difficult for you to reach the central areas in your raised bed.

#3: Install the supporting stakes in the ground

No building can stand on its own without its strong pillars that prevent it from tumbling to the ground. Similarly, the walls of your raised bed will not be able to stand on their own unless you provide some kind of support.

Therefore, you should start by driving stakes at least 12 inches into the ground on each corner of your raised bed, using a sledgehammer. The stakes should preferably be thick and strong: a good size would be 2 inches by 2 inches.

Other than that, you also need to provide support to the sides, so install stakes in the same manner keeping a distance of 5 feet between every stake on all the sides. Now the pillars of your structure are ready.

#4: Screw the wooden walls into place

Take your wooden planks or boards and make sure that they are cut to appropriate lengths so that they meet and fit comfortably with each other on the corners. Start installing them one by one, beginning with the longer sides.

Use long, galvanized screws (to prevent rusting) to attach your wooden board to each of the stakes along its length. It is up to you whether you want to use two screws per stake or just one, but the sturdier your raised bed, the better.

In this manner, install all the wooden boards, once again making sure that they fit snugly together and that there is no empty space between them (which would result in the soil and water leaking out).

#5: Fill in some soil to form the base for your raised bed

If you want to separate the soil beneath your bed with the one that you will be pouring inside, or if you simply want to give a good stabilizing layer that will keep your soil from wobbling and tumbling, you can place a layer of chicken wire at the bottom. You can also choose to skip this step altogether.

Next, pour in some soil at the base to a reasonable height so that it forms the base of your bed. If you had removed some grassy soil before installing your bed, you can put that soil back in upside down (the grass facing downwards) and the grass will rot away over time.

#6: Make up the top layer with quality topsoil and compost

The only thing remaining now is to put in the top layer of high quality soil that will house your seeds and most of the roots of the plants that you will be growing in your garden.

A general guideline is to add a 50:50 ratio of topsoil and garden (or general purpose) compost, however, if you would like to know all of your options and understand why this is important, you can take a quick detour to the next chapter where I discuss everything related to choosing the soil for your bed. If you are not in a hurry, I would suggest completing this chapter before moving on to the next!

Once you have completed all of these steps, voilà! Your wooden raised bed is ready, and you can now start worrying about planting your seeds and beginning the nurturing process. As mentioned earlier, in the next chapter we will be talking about planning your garden, so stay tuned for that. But before we head over, let's bring this chapter to a satisfactory end by going over the 8 easy steps to build a raised bed out of bricks!

8 easy steps to build a raised bed from bricks

As we've already discussed earlier, bricks can be an ideal (if you take away the cost factor) material for making your raised bed because of the durability and long life that they bring to your bed. Here are the 8 steps through which you can successfully build your own raised bed out of them!

#1: Find your spot and mark the perimeter

If you read the steps described to make a wooden raised bed, you must already know what this step is about. But if you haven't, do not worry, I won't leave you hanging for skipping over a section of this book.

The very first thing you need to do is follow the guidelines given in the section about locating your raised bed and use them to find a suitable location in your garden, or on your patio, or outside your main door, if that is where you want to make your RBG. Once you know where you will be locating it, the next step is simply to mark the perimeter of the raised bed garden with a string or anything that will stay in place until you've gotten something concrete in its place.

The perimeter will be based on the length and width of your raised bed – this could be driven by space constraints or some calculation on your part about the number of plants you want to sow, but make sure to keep the width low (less than 3 feet) so that it does not become a hassle to reach the plants in the center. Once you're done with this, you can move on to the next step.

#2: Give it a concrete foundation

You will be making a kind of wall out of bricks, and so you do not want the ground beneath all that weight to be soft and loose, lest your wall sink down into the ground or tumble forward because of weak foundations. This is why you will be making a bed of concrete to support your bricks.

Dig a pathway 20 inches deep along the perimeter (remember the string?) of your raised bed, keeping it at a width of two bricks (two is better than one). Next, line this pit with a concrete foundation up to a height of 6 inches from the base, i.e. leaving 14 inches from the surface for the bricks to fill in.

For the concrete you can use a formula of your choice, but if you are not sure, you can mix 1 part of cement with 2 and a half parts of sand and 3 and a half parts of gravel. This should get you a good strong mixture that is not too sloppy. Once you have poured in the concrete, let it dry out before moving on to the bricks.

#3: Prepare the glue that will keep the bricks stuck together

Of course I am not recommending that you use some kind of glue to bond together your bricks. The right material (and tool) for the right job is an essential rule to follow.

The formula for making the mixture of cement that will be used with your bricks is: three parts sand, one part cement, and some water to make the 'glue' into an easy to use consistency that can be applied easily on bricks and keeps them stuck together. You can also experiment with adding some plasticizer to the mixture to increase its flexibility. Now we are ready to get to the real brick-laying business.

#4: Let the bricks rise to the ground

Now you can get started with laying the bricks, keeping the course two bricks wide, making sure the bricks snug in tightly and have a good layer of cement between to hold their place. Before starting the next layer, put in place a 1-inch thick bed of cement so that the layers have a good bond between each other as well.

When you complete a course, take care of 2 things:

1. Use a level gauge to make sure that the entire course is level. This is important because a deviation in height at any point will result in a huge structural weakness that can bring your entire bed to ruin.

2. When you get finished with a layer, don't start the next layer on top by matching the positions of the bricks in the previous layer. Instead, start by keeping an offset of half a brick. This 'staggering' pattern increases the structural strength and integrity and will fortify your raised bed from most dangers.

#5: Let the bricks rise above the ground

When you are planting the layers of bricks, note that by the time you are done cementing three layers of bricks, the walls of your raised bed will have reached the ground. The next step is simply to carry on with this process until the RBG reaches your desired height, which as we've seen earlier, depends partly on the kind of plant you want to grow and partly on the conditions. Leave space for the top layer of bricks for which we will use a special kind.

#6: Make the top edge moisture-resistant and aesthetic

You should apply a complete layer of chamfered coping bricks on the top edge of your bed. This will be the last layer of your RBG, and the unique nature of these bricks will make sure to make your edges protected from any kind of damping, along with raising the visual appeal of your entire raised bed.

#7: Line the inside walls with a permeable membrane

This is an important step, because again you do not want your bricks absorbing too much water and getting all damp from the inside, because among other things, this could lead to the growth of various kinds of fungi on the insides of the bricks, which will inevitably contaminate the soil. You can either use a cellophane-based membrane to apply to the inner surface, or just properly stick a landscape fabric inside to serve as an alternative.

If you are tired, do not worry, because we are almost near the end! Your raised bed is almost ready!

#8: Fill it in with soil, topsoil, and compost

First of all, congratulations! You have (technically) completed your raised bed made out of bricks. If you've done the construction correctly, you can pat yourself on the back and sit back for years on end and watch this bed stand the test of time.

Once again, in order to complete this process, we arrive at a step which you must recall was present in the previous section on building a wooden bed. As with that one, you have to fill in the enclosed space that you have created with something that will house all of your seeds and plants.

Based on the height you have built your bed up to, you should fill approximately half of the depth with everyday soil – you could simply use the soil and earth you had dug out to make the pathway for the bricks. Once this is in place, you can then add a mixture of quality topsoil and compost to bring the soil surface up to the highest layer of bricks. As mentioned before, a useful ratio of topsoil to compost is 50:50, which will make sure that you get quality plants growing in your bed!

There you have it! You have now been made capable and equipped with all the knowledge needed to build your own raised bed: be it made out of wood, or bricks! It is now time that you start applying the knowledge that you are acquiring in this book. Of course, it is a good idea to plan everything out beforehand and gather all the materials, but if you wait for too long, you might never end up starting at all. So consider this a call to action: time to make your raised bed yourself!

This brings us to the end of a long but incredibly crucial chapter! There was a lot to take in, a lot of things to keep in mind, but safe to say if you were able to do it properly, you will by now have an amazing raised bed which is ready for planting. Let's move on to the next chapter!

Chapter 4:
How to plan your garden

The quality of your soil, the level of nutrients that it contains, the amount of moisture that it can retain – all of these are important factors which affect the quality of plants that you will be able to grow. Therefore, it is important that you are able to put in good quality soil into your raised bed and know when and how to replenish it, so that you can put in the nutrients that get sucked by the plants.

In this chapter, I will tell you all you need to know to make good decisions regarding the quality of soil that you put in your raised bed garden. We will discuss the kinds of soil you can encounter, how to test the quality of your soil, the difference between compost and peat moss, how you can use these to fertilize your soil, and what is the best way to plant seeds and seedlings. Let's begin with the types of soils [5].

The types of soil that can go into your RBG

If you go to a garden center to buy soil for your raised bed garden, you will find yourself faced with a number of different kinds of soil which will leave you scratching your head, trying to figure out what will work best for you. Learn about the types of soil beforehand so that you can easily select the one that suits you best.

#1: Garden soil

Garden soil happens to be a dense and heavy soil which primarily consists of topsoil mixed in with other minerals and materials suitable for growing vegetables, trees, and shrubs. This might not be the best option to use in a raised bed because of its density, since it will get compacted very quickly. If you still want to use it, make sure to amend this type of soil with compost annually so that the soil does not become devoid of any nutrients.

#2: Potting mix

Potting mix is a lightweight soil that consists of materials like sphagnum moss, compost, and bark. It is also sterilized so that it does not allow the growth of fungi inside your RBG. What makes this kind of soil suited for use in a RBG is its light weight, which prevents compaction of the soil and allows for good drainage and aeration, allowing good room for the roots to blossom. It is also a good choice if you want to grow vegetables, just make sure you include some compost or peat moss in your RBG when you are laying down this soil.

#3: Raised garden bed mix

As the name suggests, this is the soil that garden centers make specifically for use in RBGs. So if you can find this near you in a garden center, you don't need to look for anything else. However, you can also make this yourself because most garden centers simply make this by mixing 50% of potting mix with 50% of garden soil.

#4: Topsoil

Although you will find topsoil mixed in with a lot of other varieties, you will never find anyone recommending that you fill your RBG with topsoil only. The reason behind this is that topsoil is merely the soil taken from the 'top' layer of the Earth and so contains hardly any nutrients and is usually quite dense in itself. For this reason, it is mostly used as a 'filler' and 'conditioner' and mixed in with soil of much higher quality in order to arrive at a balanced combination.

That brings us to the end of the discussion on the types of soil that you will encounter. You must be wondering by now, what are these 'nutrients' in the soil that everyone keeps talking about? What is this 'pH' that everyone keeps trying to maintain? These are important questions for which you should know the answers, because these determine what you can and cannot grow in your garden.

Soil pH and nutrients

Acidic of alkaline?

Based on the concentration of minerals in your soil, your soil could either be acidic or alkaline. If your soil has a pH value (a measurement of acidity/alkalinity) of less than 7, your soil is more on the acidic side. The closer you get to 1, the more acidic it becomes. Inversely, if your soil has a pH value of more than 7, it is said to be alkaline, with the alkalinity increasing as you get closer to 14.

Now you must be thinking – why does it matter what pH my soil is? The answer to that is that it matters because certain plants and vegetables need a certain kind of soil pH in order to grow. For example, most plants and vegetables prefer acidic soil (i.e. with a pH less than 7) in order to grow well. You need to be able to maintain the pH level of your soil to make sure your plants don't betray you.

What are the essential nutrients?

The essential nutrients that a plant needs are shortened into a convenient acronym called NPK [6], after the symbols used for these elements in the periodic table. N stands for Nitrogen, P for Phosphorus, and K for Potassium. These are the nutrients everyone tries to make sure are in healthy levels in your soil. Why is that?

Nitrogen is the nutrient responsible for the 'green' in the plants. It is needed by the plants if they are to be as green as possible, so you can tell if your leaves have become dull and yellow that your soil lacks Nitrogen. Phosphorus contributes to the healthy and full development of flowers, fruits, and roots, and so without enough P in your soil, you will notice stunted development in each of these. Finally, Potassium, or K, supports the basic functions of plants including protein synthesis and photosynthesis, and so is one of the building blocks for every plant.

It is always important to keep a track of the pH -and nutrients- level of your soil so that you can correct it when required. Veteran gardeners can tell just by taking a short look at the soil, but for the more amateurs among us, there are home testing kits available which you can easily acquire and use once a year to run the diagnostics of your RBG soil. These tests will tell you what is lacking and what is in excess, and give you the right direction to improve the quality of your soil and ensure a healthy and plentiful yield for the next growing seasons.

Compost and peat moss – essential partners for your soil

When you buy the right kind of soil for your RBG, it contains all the nutrients that your seeds and plants will need to grow well. In some cases, it is still recommended to reinforce this soil with compost or peat moss when you are starting out with your RBG.

However, 'amending' your soil becomes necessary once you have gone through one or two harvesting seasons. This is because the plants you are growing are sucking the nutrients from the soil to grow, and so within a year or two, your soil will be left deficient in nutrients. It won't be able to grow healthy plants at all if you do not replenish it.

In order to do this replenishing, two kinds of materials are often used – compost and peat moss. Let's look at what these are.

What is compost?

Chances are that even if you don't have any prior experience of gardening, you still know what compost is and what it is used for. However, if you have been living in a cave for most of your life, don't worry, I've got your back.

Compost is what you get once organic matter decays. It is incredibly rich in nutrients, making it an ideal candidate to replenish the health of your soil. It is widely available and comes in many forms: you can find composted animal manures such as cow, chicken, and rabbit, and even composted plant material. Some people make their own compost from kitchen and food waste that gets accumulated and decomposed over time.

Compost is cheap and contains numerous microorganisms that help with improving the quality of the soil around it. Aside from being an excellent organic fertilizer, there are several downsides to it as well: compost may get compacted over time, reducing the aeration and drainage in your soil, and it may even contain certain weed seeds.

What is peat moss?

Peat moss is another form of compost – just a very specific kind. Whereas compost consists of a wide range of organic matter, peat moss consists only of decomposed moss (as the name suggests) and is excavated from peat bogs, or wetlands.

Another key difference between peat moss and normal compost is that the decomposition takes place without the presence of air and so the process takes hundreds of years. This is why peat moss is not so readily available – it is more like a mineral that is mined from the Earth.

However, when it comes to function, it is an incredible source of nutrients for the soil, and possesses qualities that make it better than compost – it can retain moisture several times its weight, it lasts for years on end, is an ideal mixture to use for your starting soil, and it is sterilized so it won't contain any harmful organisms or weeds.

One of the biggest downsides is that peat moss is expensive, and excavating it from the Earth releases a lot of carbon dioxide into the air, contributing to the global carbon footprint. These are the reasons people generally prefer using peat moss in special circumstances, i.e. when laying the soil in the bed or helping the seedlings sprout out.

Which one should you use?

This is a question that must be playing around in your mind. Which of the above two should you use, then? There is no clear binary answer to this. The answer depends on several factors [7].

The first factor is the preferred pH level of the plants that you are growing. Peat moss makes the soil slightly acidic, and so it is an ideal amendment material if you are looking to grow plants that thrive in slightly acidic soil. However, if your plants prefer more alkaline soil, you are better off sticking with compost. The next chapters will fill you in on the kinds of plants that prefer either acidic or alkaline soil, so you should stay tuned for that.

For now, there is another strategy that you can use that will serve you well. When you are starting out and just filling your RBG with soil, it is best if you can get your hands on some peat moss and use it to enrich your soil. This will give your soil a good start and ensure that you start out with strong yields and harvests.

At all other times when you are looking to replenish your soil's state of nutrients, you should use compost because of its easy availability and environmentally-friendly nature. If you follow this strategy, you will be able to make the best use of both of these soil-enhancing substances.

When should I add the compost every year?

I've already told you that you have to add compost to your soil every year to make sure it does not get starved of nutrients and is able to deliver bumper crops year on year. Now I will give you specific details on when you should be doing it [8].

The general guideline is that you should mix compost into your soil before each planting season. You could have one or multiple planting seasons in the same year based on your geography, so let's look at how that will work out.

If you live in cooler climates such as the Northeast or Midwest U.S.A., U.K., or Canada, you will have one planting season per year which will be from late spring to early fall. The best way for you to do your composting would be to lay partially decomposed compost on your RBGs after your harvest (in fall before the ground freezes) so that once planting season rolls around, your soil will have absorbed the nutrients from the compost and will be ready.

If you live in a warmer climate, you will have year-round gardening and will come across two planting seasons – one during the cooler climate and the other during the summer. The general schedule for these two seasons is like this: Since the cooler season spans from mid-September till April, add the compost at the end of August or start of September. For the warmer seasons (which runs from mid-February through March into the hotter months), you should aim to have applied finished compost by the time spring rolls around.

If you follow these guidelines year-on-year, you can be sure that you will continue to have excellent yield after yield.

From seed to seedling and plant

There are two ways you can get your seed started on the journey of growth – indoor and outdoor sowing [9]. With indoor sowing, you normally provide controlled conditions for your seed so that it has the maximum chances of sprouting in the most critical time, and then you later transplant it into your garden. With outdoor sowing, as the name suggests, you skip this step and directly sow your seed in your garden.

The choice of whether to start with indoor or directly go to the outdoor part depends on the round-the-year climate in your area and the plant that you want to grow. Here are some factors that will help you make your decision.

You will get a head start if you grow your seeds indoors because you will be able to start earlier and have seedlings ready to be transplanted by the time the planting season rolls around.

Moreover, you can comfortably control the temperature, humidity, and moisture that the seeds are getting when you are keeping them indoors. However, the one problem that you will face is that certain vegetables such as carrots, beets, turnips, and parsnips do not respond well to being transplanted. Given their cold-resistant nature, they are better off planted directly.

Harden your seeds with indoor sowing

The main benefit of indoor sowing is that it helps you 'harden' your seeds, i.e. prepares them to withstand the force of the elements which it will face once it has been sent out into the world. You do not have to do this with seedlings that you get from a nursery (those are ready to be transplanted), but if you are getting seeds or seedlings from a greenhouse, this is an important step.

Leave the seed or seedling in a warm container full of nutrient-rich soil which you will have to keep watering frequently to keep up the moisture content of the soil. Do this for a few days. Carry this on till the sowing time if the plant is shade-friendly, but start exposing the plant to the sunlight in small incremental doses if your plant is to grow in a sunny spot.

This will make sure these get hardened according to the conditions that they will face.

Avoid leaving them inside for too much hardening because it may result in your plants bolting, i.e. sprouting out prematurely and not really growing to full potential.

When you feel that it is time to transplant them, prepare the soil in your RBG by digging away the areas where you want to place the roots. The best practice is to make sure your soil is well-composted and has enough moisture when you are planting, and do the transplanting in the afternoon, to allow the seedlings some time to get used to their new habitat before they start dealing with sunlight. Use a shade if necessary, ease them into their new surroundings. Now you need to take care of them as you would any plant.

Skip the indoor step and sow them directly

If you live in a place where the summer season is reasonably long, you do not have to start growing your seeds indoors – you can plant them directly into your RBG. This is especially the case for vegetables that have large seeds and grow fast such as corn, melons, squash, beans, and peas.

Before direct sowing, make sure that the soil has dried out and that it is warm enough for your seeds. You do not want your seeds to die prematurely. The choice of how you want to pattern your plants in your RBG is up to you, just make sure that the seeds are safely ensconced inside the soil.

Grooming the seedlings

Once your seeds have started to grow and sprout out, they will produce the seed leaves (the first set of leaves) followed by the second set of true leaves. This is when you should thin them out in order to prevent overcrowding, which will ultimately affect how well your seeds are able to sit inside.

Congratulations! You have everything sorted out now – your raised bed, the soil, composting, and planting the seeds. The only remaining step that will formally make you a raised bed gardener, is deciding what you will plant. The next three chapters will not only guide you on how you can choose your plant, but also tell you about all the vegetables and plants that you can grow. Let's carry right on!

Chapter 5:
Factors that determine what and how you plant

When you have finally gotten your raised bed and soil just right, you will have to sit down and figure out what you want to plant. The process, however, is not as simple as just buying all the vegetable varieties that you can find and sowing them in your garden, hoping for everything to turn out well. Turns out, you need to plan the layout of your garden (take a pencil and start drawing on a piece of paper) based on a number of factors, which we will now discuss.

Season

You cannot expect to randomly sow a certain plant at any time of the year and expect it to be harvest-ready in a couple of months if you do not take into consideration the season that you are growing that plant in. As it happens, most plants are not able to survive either harsh summers or frosty winters, and therefore you need to first figure out which season you will be planting in. The choice of what to plant changes based on the season you are targeting. In any case, the following table will quell all your queries because I've divided the two major seasons and the plants to grow in each [10].

Spring and Fall vegetables	Summer vegetables
• Broccoli	• Beans
• Brussels sprouts	• Corn
• Cabbage	• Cucumber
• Collards	• Eggplant
• English peas	• Gourds
• Kale	• Melons
• Kohlrabi	• Okra
• Leeks	• Peppers
• Mustard greens	• Pumpkins

• Parsley • Radish • Spinach • Turnip	• Southern peas • Summer squash • Sweet potatoes • Tomatoes

Preference for sunlight and water

Even though we learned in school that plants function based on photosynthesis, for which they need sunlight and water, we didn't really figure out that the reality was more nuanced than that. Some plants require a lot more sunlight and water than others, whereas some will survive even in drought-like conditions. Thus, it is clear that different plants have different preferences, and whether you plant them, where you plant them, and when you plant them is determined by those preferences.

It would take up too much space to list down the preferences of each of the vegetables and herbs mentioned up till now, so to make it easier for you, I've made chapters 6 and 7 about the simplest vegetables and herbs to grow, making sure to include the preferences of each in the descriptions. Do not forget to follow those guidelines, unless you want your plants to suffer at the hands of unfavorable conditions.

Location

Not all plants grow to the same height. Some climb up into the sky while others spread themselves on the ground. It is important to account for this difference when making the layout for your garden, because you want to take care of the aesthetics of your RBG and make sure that the taller plants don't end up blocking the sunlight needed by the smaller ones.

As a general rule, if your RBG has a path going around it (i.e. if it is visible from multiple sides), it is best to keep the taller plants in the middle. This means that the plants next to the tall ones will receive some shade at some point in the day, so you should place the more shade-friendly ones like lettuce next to the tall varieties, making sure those that need adequate sunlight are placed close to the edges.

Companion Vegetables

Companion planting is a concept that gets touted as conventional wisdom, but the truth is that science has begun to lend quite a bit of weight to its practices. The general idea is that there are groups of plants which are much better suited to being together, i.e. they complement each other – one improves the soil for the other while another attracts pollinators, one keeps pests away while the other provides shade. There are various combinations to look out for, and I've compiled them all in the following table [11]. Remember, just like some plants enhance the growth of their companions, some other ones might even be harmful, so choose accordingly!

Plant	Good companions	Keep away from
Tomatoes	Basil, marigold, asparagus, carrots, celery, onions, lettuce, parsley, spinach	Cabbage, beets, peas, fennel, dill, rosemary, potatoes
Peppers	Basil, onions, spinach, tomatoes	Beans
Green beans	Corn, marigold, nasturtiums, rosemary, summer savory, broccoli, Brussels sprouts, cucumbers, peas, potatoes, radishes	Beets, onion family
Cucumbers	Marigold, nasturtium, beans, celery, corn, lettuce, dill, peas, radishes	Aromatic herbs (e.g. sage)
Onions	Carrots, beets, cabbage, lettuce, parsnips, tomatoes, marjoram, savory, rosemary	Asparagus, beans, peas

Lettuce	Mint, chives, garlic, beans, beet, broccoli, carrots, corn, peas, radishes, marigold	Parsley
Zucchini/Summer squash	Corn, beans, peas, radishes, dill, marigold	Potatoes
Carrots	Tomatoes, leeks, rosemary, chive, sage	Coriander, dill, parsnips
Radishes	Cucumbers, carrots, onions, beets, cabbage, kale, lettuce, spinach, squash	Hyssop
Sweet corn	Green beans, cucumbers, peas, pumpkin, melons, zucchini	Tomatoes

Companion planting is a very extensive and articulated argument. From this paragraph you can get a general idea of what companion planting is and how it works, plus some suggestions of good and bad companions among your plants. If you may want to go a little deeper in this fascinating world you may be interested in my book on this same topic: **Companion Planting**: *A beginners guide to companion planting secrets. Why vegetables, herbs and flowers can be good friends (or bitter enemies), and how this can help you growing an health organic garden*

The above table and the discussion on how climate and location matter will have cleared the path before you, making you ready to now take the (calculated) leap of faith and select your vegetables and herbs, making the layout for your garden. The next two chapters will walk you through the simplest and easiest-to-grow veggies and herbs that you should consider starting out with, along with some guidelines to take care of. Keep going, you are almost done!

Chapter 6:
the 5 Best vegetables to grow

It can be difficult to decide which vegetables to grow in your raised bed garden, given the hundreds of varieties that you will find in the markets. However, it is also true that there are certain veggies that are more suited to RBGs, and a lot easier to grow than others. In this chapter, I will take you through the 5 vegetables that you should seriously consider starting out with [12]!

#1: Tomatoes

Tomatoes are among the most commonly-grown vegetables that you can find. However, the larger varieties will generally take a lot of time and effort, so I would suggest you stick to cherry tomatoes when you start out because these will start producing even two months after you've planted them into your RBG.

Some varieties for you to try out include Sun Gold, Jasper, and Sunrise Bumble Bee. When growing tomatoes, you have to provide support to the plant by driving stakes into the soil and hanging your plants to it. This is important if you want your tomatoes to grow healthy and well.

#2: Cucumbers

Cucumbers are universally known for the crunch and cool they bring to the lives of people, especially in hot summers. You will be delighted to know that cucumbers are well-suited for RBGs, and you can quite easily get away with direct seeding them into the ground. If you can fulfill the basics (provide plenty of compost and frequent watering), you will find an excellent harvest of cucumbers waiting to reach your stomach!

If you are strained for space, you can try growing varieties like Pick-a-Bushel, Saladmore Bush, and Spacemaster, but if you don't have to worry about that, you can go for varieties like Suyu Long, Lemon, and Diva.

#3: Garlic

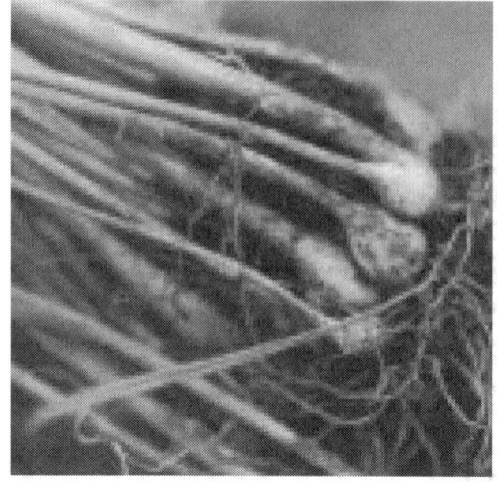

Garlic is one of the easiest vegetables to grow, so much that people call it the 'plant it and forget about it' type. All you have to do is designate an area for your garlic, plant it during autumn, and add some compost or mulch to the surface to give the soil some reinforcement.

After that, you can pretty much forget about it until next summer rolls around. The sign you should be on the lookout for is the partial yellowing of leaves which will tell you that it is now ready for harvest. Take the plants out and leave them to dry for a while before removing the bulbs for use.

#4: Leaf lettuce

Leaf lettuce, much like garlic, is another one of those vegetables which are quite easy and quick to grow (and munch on). You can directly sow the seeds in your RBG, making sure to plan for six-inch wide beds, and helping the soil retain good moisture until the plant crops out of the soil.

After that, you can harvest these leafy greens once they are about two to four inches long. A better idea would be to cut off the leaves from the sides and edges because this allows the center of the plant to continue growing, extending the harvesting period. Some notable seed varieties for you to try include the Red Salad Bowl, Red Sails, and Black Seeded Simpson.

#5: Summer squash

The squash is a vegetable that truly embodies the concept of 'bang for your buck'. Even if you grow a single plant, you will have more squash than you will be able to eat! The way to go about with squashes is that you can directly sow the seed in your RBG, making sure to provide adequate compost to the plant.

After that, you can monitor its growth and harvest it at the right time, to maximize quality and flavor. For the round varieties, you can harvest them when the fruits are two to three inches in diameter. As for zucchini, harvest when they are four to six inches long.

There you have it: the 5 best vegetables to grow in your raised bed garden. Of course, this list is not all-encompassing. There are more vegetables to grow than you can count on your fingers, but especially when someone is starting out, it is best to stick to the simpler and easier varieties to get some good experience under your belt. That will leave you with enough confidence to then venture on towards more difficult ones.

Chapter 7:
the 6 best herbs to grow

Imagine stepping out of your kitchen and being welcomed by fresh aromas coming from a variety of herbs growing in your garden. Imagine seasoning your food with a different herb every day – this is what you will get if you plant herbs in your RBG, and I highly recommend that you do. It is simple and easy – let's take a look at the 6 best herbs you can grow.

#1: Basil

Basil is one of those herbs best suited for round-the-year growth and harvesting, taking up little effort from you. It thrives in sunlight, so you have to make sure that you plant it on a spot that receives adequate amounts of it. Because it is exposed to sunlight, you also have to take care that the soil retains good moisture and drainage throughout.

If you can do as much, then you can sit back and relax the rest of the time because Basil will be around for you all year round. Keep harvesting the leaves from time to time, this forces the plant to keep on growing. Finally, cut away any flowers if they show up because they take the flavor away from the leaves.

#2: Greek oregano

Everybody loves to sprinkle oregano on to their homemade pizza and pasta – it is an excellent companion for most dishes. What makes this even better is that it will grow enthusiastically if you plant it inside your RBG, just making sure that it gets enough water. Although Greek oregano is that most commonly grown variety, you can also try Syrian oregano, a more tender kind of oregano.

#3: Rosemary

If you want to improve the taste of your potato and chicken dishes, rosemary is an ideal candidate. With its exquisite aroma, it can add a much-desired depth to any dish that it gets on. Just like oregano, rosemary can grow annually, and so it is very much possible for you to manage its growth in a way that you never have to plant it again. Just don't end up watering it too much – the idea is to moisturize, not drown.

#4: Thyme

Thyme is a rather tough herb: it can withstand spells of drought and neglect without withering away. Because of this quality, it prefers to thrive in soil that is not very well moisturized. This low-maintenance feature makes thyme an ideal herb for planting in any garden, especially on the edges of a RBG because the spreading leaves covering the sides is a beautiful sight to behold.

#5: Mint

Mint is one of the most widely known and used herbs around the world. From chewing gums to margaritas, you will find its flavor being extracted for all sorts of edible and drinkable items. The good part is that you can grow it easily in your RBG as well – mint grows quite aggressively so the confines of your RBG will put a limit on it, allowing you to control how far it spreads.

Do not forget to give it a good watering and composting from time to time, because it prefers to stay moisturized and nutrient-rich. You can try out varieties like peppermint, spearmint, and even chocolate mint.

#6: Parsley

Parsley is another herb that you will find quite frequently used for culinary purposes – it is not uncommon to sprinkle a bit of parsley on your food to give its taste an instant upgrade. It can be quite easy to grow if you can keep the soil moisturized and healthy (through sufficient composting). Moreover, it is a Sun-friendly herb, so you are better off putting it in some good sunlight.

Those were the 6 herbs that you must try out at some point in your RBG. The days of having to buy processed herbs from the supermarket are gone – now you can find them growing just behind your kitchen, all at your disposal.

Chapter 8:

Importance of post-harvest care

A lot of people fall into the trap of thinking that they've already put in all the effort that was required, they have already made sure the plants had the perfect condition to grow in, and now once the plants have grown and are ready for harvest, they can harvest and eat them and sit back and relax.

The problem is that only part of it is true: you can indeed harvest your hard-earned vegetables and herbs and then have a feast at your place, but after that, you cannot sit back and relax, especially if you plan to continue to grow plants in your RBG.

Your garden will not be very forgiving if you forget about it until the next planting season comes around – you have to put in some effort after the harvest as well, helping the depleted garden get back to its natural health. In this chapter I am going to talk about the 7 aspects of post-harvest care [13]. Let's begin.

#1: Finish your harvest

When you feel that the time is right to bring your summer garden to an end, make sure that you have harvested everything from it before you proceed forward. Fruits like tomatoes can ripen up even after harvest so there is no need to wait. As for the herbs, you can harvest and dry them so that you can use them throughout winter, even freezing them if you intend to hold onto them for longer.

#2: Remove the summer and diseased plants, and weeds

Once you have removed all the fruit and vegetables from the plants, you should remove the summer plants as well and put them in your compost bin, they will be useful when the next season rolls around. As for the diseased plants, remove them but do not let them go near your compost bin – send them straight to the garbage. Removing all these plants will expose a lot of hidden weeds – use your hand or a hoe to turn them out and dispose of them, especially if they have seeds.

#3: Replenish your soil's nutrients

If you want to continue growing vegetables year after year, the best thing you can do is take care of the health of your soil. Every time you pass through a planting season, the fruits and veggies suck out a lot of nutrition from the soil – it is your responsibility to replenish all that is lost. There are two ways to do this.

The first involves the use of compost. This is a more favorable option because there is a lot you can control. Apply a good layer of compost on the top of your soil and use a garden tool to till it over so that the compost gets mixed well with your soil.

The second method involves planting cover crops. These are crops (not necessarily meant for harvesting) which help in improving the nutrient balance in the soil and suppressing weed growth. Examples include rye grass, oats, barley, and clover.

#4: Cover the surface

Unless you are planting a cover crop, you should spread some mulch over the surface of your RBG. This will prevent any weeds from popping up while keeping the soil warm and moist.

#5: Give the perennials their due

This is a nice time to strip down your perennials, cutting away the weaker sprouts and branches, leaving only the healthy ones. This will reinvigorate the growth of your perennial edibles. To bring some protection from winter, you can add some mulch (straw or bark) to the surface near these perennials, even sprinkle some compost to help the soil remain healthy.

#6: Your garden tools need your attention

All this gardening and planting would not have been possible were it not for all of your garden tools. If you do not stack them away with the proper treatment, there is a high chance you will find them diseased and rusted when you next bring them out. The way to deal with this is to dip all the metal parts in bleach and cover them up with some oil at the end to prevent rusting and disease. This will make sure that when you bring them out in the next season, they are just like you left them.

#7: Prepare for next year

Once you've rested yourself a bit, you should get out a pen and paper and do some analysis. Figure out which plants were successful and which were not, what mistakes did you make this time around that you want to fix for the future, what aspect of layout do you need to change, and whether your RBG will benefit from some pollinator-attracting plants around the edges. Answering questions like these will help you improve your techniques and practices, helping you to get better yields year after year.

Chapter 9:
Protecting the plants from pests

It often happens that a diligent gardener will spend hours and days on end taking care of his garden and vegetables, finding that they are growing well, imagining the rewards that he will reap when the harvest season comes round, only to find that all his hard work has been laid to waste by pests. This happens to a lot of people, and you may be driven into thinking that maybe you will need pesticides for your garden to protect it.

However, I am here to tell you that you do not need to use pesticides – even if they are 'organic'. This is because even organic pesticides contain harmful materials and have a history of causing poisoning among people. Instead, there are strategies that you can use to prevent the appearance and spread of pests in your plants, and in this chapter I will talk about 5 of these strategies [14].

#1: Gather a team of beneficial insects to help you out!

Did you know that there are certain insects, the beneficial kind, that will gladly munch on the pests that terrorize your garden, as if you hired them for the job? Indeed, insects such as lacewings, ladybugs, pirate bugs, parasitic wasps, and damsel bugs eat pests for food so if you have them lying around in your garden, they will act as natural and safe pesticides for you.

The question you will have is: how do I encourage more beneficial insects to make their homes in my garden? There are several ways to do this. You will need to provide them with protein-rich pests to consume, but also some rich nectar which will come about from a certain kind of flowers that you will have to plant. Examples of such plants include sunflowers, daisies, lace flowers, buckwheats, and phacelias. The more pest-munching insects you have, the more you can be confident that there is someone else looking after your plants.

#2: Choose pest-resistant varieties

Your plants do not have to completely be at the mercy of pests. There are quite a lot of varieties now available that are 'resistant' to pests. All you have to do is do some good research and seek such varieties when you are going to buy seeds.

For example, if your squash plants are at the mercy of bugs, you can go for the 'Butternut' and 'Royal Acorn' varieties that will resist them. If your potatoes are being plagued by irritating beetles, plant the 'King Harry' potato that has hairy leaves and does not allow beetles to eat them.

#3: Install physical barriers

Pests will not be able to eat up your plants if they cannot access them in the first place, right? This is another way you can protect your garden from pests, i.e. by installing some kind of cover on your plants that blocks all the pathways that a pest can use to get to your precious vegetables.

A good option is to use a floating row cover which is a lightweight fabric supported by wire hoops and attaches to the ground (or the sides of your raised bed) on all ends, effectively blocking access of pests to the plants. Although this will work like a charm, you need to be careful about still allowing pollinators to do their job properly, so you might have to remove these covers when the time is right.

#4: Intercropping will confuse the pests

This technique has garnered much interest and research in recent times. The idea behind intercropping is that you increase the diversity of the plants in your raised beds, i.e. instead of planting a single vegetable in a row, you mix it up with multiple kinds of vegetables, herbs, and flowers, leading to a diverse garden for yourself.

Although this is still being investigated, the way this stops pests from finding host plants in your garden is that it 'confuses' them. A pest cannot see and identify the plant like we can, so it must visit the same variety a few times to actually decide to settle down for some lunch. If it keeps going back to a different plant, it will not be able to make this decision. So embrace diversity in your own garden and help it keep away the pests!

#5: Focus on the health of your plants

Just like we emphasize a healthy and fit body in order to protect ourselves from diseases and bacteria, we should realize that this concept applies equally well to the world of plants – after all, they are living organisms as well, despite being a lot less complex than us humans!

Therefore, if you focus on maintaining the health of your plants, making sure they are well-fed, receiving the necessary nutrition, and not in stressful conditions, they will automatically become unattractive to pests and will be able to better deal with them in the case of an attack, utilizing their 'chemical defense systems'. So follow the advice given in chapter 4 and make sure that your soil is kept moist and nutritious, and that your plants are kept in the condition that they best thrive in!

These were the 5 strategies that, if implemented properly, will make you forget that pesticides even exist in this world – you will have effectively prevented pests from laying waste to all of your hard work.

Chapter 10:
5 Common mistakes and how to avoid them

Despite reading through books and articles, planning for days on end, and acquiring the best materials and seeds, you may still be finding yourself struggling to get good yields with raised bed gardening. This may simply be because you are making some of the common mistakes that even long-time gardeners end up making when switching over to RBG. In this chapter, I will take you through the 5 common mistakes that people tend to make and how you can avoid them [15].

#1: **Your raised beds are too wide**

Raised beds are designed in a way that they prevent soil compaction – you do not have to step on the soil surface, and this helps the roots grow comfortably. However, if you end up making your raised bed too wide (mistakenly thinking that it won't be a problem), you might in the end find yourself stepping onto the soil in order to reach the central areas.

This defeats the purpose of the raised bed and will lead to soil compaction, damaging the roots, preventing their growth, and ultimately leading to lower yields. Therefore, the best idea is to keep your raised beds to a maximum width of four feet, even sticking to three feet if you want the process to be a whole lot comfortable.

#2: You didn't plan the irrigation well

Because of the better drainage characteristics, you will find that RBGs require frequent watering in order to keep the soil moisturized. This can become a hassle if you did not make proper arrangements for the irrigation of your beds.

You can do all right with a simple watering can, but it can quickly become inefficient if you have multiple raised beds, because you will have to refill it repeatedly. Therefore, I recommend having your raised beds close to a source of water so that you do not have to take long trips just to refill your can. A better idea would be to install a hose pipe on the water source that can access all the raised beds. This will ultimately make the process of watering much more convenient for you.

#3: The material of your RBG is unsafe

Although I've stressed on this already during the entire book, this point warrants attention over here because people often end up falling into this trap. It is always a bad idea to use pressure-treated wood, especially if it was manufactured before 2003 because back then, the wood was treated with copper arsenate, a chemical that can leach into your soil and get into your digestive system through the vegetables you grow.

It is best to use non-pressure treated wood to make your raised bed, or better, recycle wood that you have that is being used for some other purpose. If you must use pressure-treated wood, make sure it was manufactured after 2003, because treatment practices have gotten quite safe since then.

#4: The soil lacks nutrients

As I've already stressed quite a bit in chapter 4 of this book, the quality of your soil, its pH level, and the nutrients that it contains matter a lot to the overall development of your plants, and if you get the combination wrong or if something is missing from your plants, you will ultimately pay the price in the form of a low yield of stunted growth.

Therefore, you need to understand the different types of soils that you can put inside your RBG and the right combination that works – I've discussed all of this in detail in chapters 3 and 4, but for your ease, here is a quick recap: unless you can find the 'raised bed garden soil' which is mixed up for the purpose, you should go with 50% of garden soil mixed up with 50% of potting mix. This will give you enough aeration and drainage to allow for healthy plants.

#5: RBGs are placed too close to each other

One of the reasons people set out trying raised bed gardening is the ease, comfort, and efficiency that comes with managing bordered enclosures containing all of your plants. However, this can quickly become an uncomfortable experience if you forget to leave sufficient space in between your raised beds to allow you to weed, sow, water, and harvest. Some people often end up leaving only a foot between their raised beds, realizing later that the little space is insufficient for tending to the plants comfortably or hauling in their wheelbarrows.

Therefore, the right guideline for you is that you should focus on keeping about 2 to 3 feet between your raised beds. This will be sufficient for you to bring your wheelbarrow in, or even put in place a stool if you would like to sit on it while you tend to your garden.

Those were the five common mistakes that people tend to make when they are trying to grow plants in a raised bed. I hope this condensed list helps you avoid these problems and make your RBG experience a successful one!

Conclusion

My main intention behind writing this book was to provide you with an easy to read encyclopedia that will lay everything out clearly in front of you so that you can get started on your raised bed gardening journey. I sincerely hope that the information I have included was useful to you and helped you in getting comfortable with this useful gardening technique.

Remember, you can come back to this book whenever you feel that you need some guidance – I am confident that it will not disappoint you! With that, I wish you the best of luck as you set out to own what you eat and develop the important skill of self-sufficiency!

Others from Chauncey Cruz Jr.

If you enjoyed Raised Bed Gardening, please also check for

Square Foot Gardening

An easy guide to get started on the path of food self-sufficiency. Build your own raised bed, and learn everything about urban and vertical gardening, and mini-farming skills

Companion Planting

A beginners guide to companion planting secrets. Why vegetables, herbs and flowers can be good friends (or bitter enemies), and how this can help you grow an health organic garden

References

[1] [Online]. Available: https://www.miraclegro.com/en-us/library/raised-bed-gardening/what-raised-bed-anyway.

[2] [Online]. Available: https://www.allotment-garden.org/gardening-information/raised-beds/.

[3] [Online]. Available: https://learn.eartheasy.com/articles/10-excellent-reasons-to-use-raised-beds-in-your-garden/.

[4] [Online]. Available: https://extension.uga.edu/publications/detail.html?number=C1027-3&title=Raised%20Beds%20vs.%20In-Ground%20Gardens.

[5] [Online]. Available: https://ecogardensystems.com/the-ultimate-guide-to-raised-bed-garden-soil/.

[6] [Online]. Available: https://www.groworganic.com/blogs/articles/home-soil-test.

[7] [Online]. Available: https://www.sundaygardener.net/differences-between-peat-moss-and-compost/.

[8] [Online]. Available: https://www.dummies.com/home-garden/green-living/when-to-add-compost-to-your-garden-beds/.

[9] [Online]. Available: https://www.dummies.com/home-garden/gardening/planting-vegetables-from-seed-and-seedling/.

[10] [Online]. Available: https://bonnieplants.com/gardening/which-veggies-for-which-season/.

[11] [Online]. Available: https://www.farmersalmanac.com/companion-planting-guide-31301.

[12] [Online]. Available: https://savvygardening.com/easiest-vegetables-to-grow/.

[13] [Online]. Available: https://www.houzz.com/magazine/what-to-do-in-your-edible-garden-after-the-summer-harvest-stsetivw-vs~113655238.

[14] [Online]. Available: https://savvygardening.com/preventing-pests-in-your-garden/.

[15] [Online]. Available: https://journeywithjill.net/gardening/2018/02/13/7-common-mistakes-in-raised-bed-gardening/.

[16] [Online]. Available: https://en.wikipedia.org/wiki/Raised-bed_gardening.

Printed in Great Britain
by Amazon